CW00701124

The Official
MANCHEST
Annual 2011

Written by David Clayton, Designed by Simon Thorley

A Grange Publication

© 2010. Published by Grange Communications Ltd., Edinburgh,
under licence from Manchester City Football Club. Printed in the EU.

Photographs © Press Association Images
& Manchester City Football Club

ISBN 978-1-907104-68-8

£7.99

Contents

Roberto's Message

When I was a young boy growing up in Italy, the only thing I wanted to be was a footballer.
I would play at school with my friends and then go out on the field with my father when I returned home and play until it was time for dinner.

My team was Juventus, but the town I lived in was a long way from Turin and my father and I had to travel for many hours on a coach to watch them play – but it was worth it!

Every Juventus player was my hero and I wanted to be just like they were and that meant practising all the time, eating the right food, working hard at school and getting plenty of sleep.

Things went well for me and eventually I began playing professionally and I was lucky enough to enjoy a long career and be involved in many cup finals and league titles – but I had to work hard for the success I had.

Now I am at Manchester City and I'm sure that our players are all your heroes, just as the Juventus players were mine.

Some of you may live close to our stadium and others may have to travel for many hours – just as I did – to come and watch the team play.

I would like to thank every one of you for your support – it means so much to myself and the team and we will be trying as hard as we can to win every game we play to ensure you enjoy your visit.

We are building a very strong team here at City and I think there will be league titles and trophies in the years to come.

There has never been a more exciting time to support this club - you are our fans of the future – so thanks again for your support and enjoy the Official 2011 Manchester City FC Annual.

See you at the game!

Roberto Mancini

Season Review 2009/10

City began the season with a 2-0 win at Blackburn with new boy Emmanuel Adebayor taking just three minutes to find the net on his debut. Stephen Ireland added a second as manager Mark Hughes saw his team make the perfect start to the season.

In fact, August proved to be perfect in every way. With Gareth Barry, Kolo Toure and Carlos Tevez fitting into the side well, three more victories were recorded that month. Adebayor's goal was enough to give City a 1-0 win over Wolves; Crystal Palace were beaten 2-0 in the Carling Cup and Adebayor struck his third successive Premier League winner with the only goal of the game at Portsmouth.

But there was even better to come as the Blues began September with a stunning 4-2 win over Arsenal at the City of Manchester Stadium. Goals from – who else? – Adebayor, Micah Richards, Shaun Wright-Phillips and Craig Bellamy sent the 47,339 fans home extremely happy after they had witnessed their team dismantle one of the title favourites.

The first Manchester derby of the season was hugely controversial, with City fighting back from behind three times only to lose to a goal that many felt should never have stood. With all the added time played and the score 3-3, the referee allowed United another minute or so during which Michael Owen prodded home the winner.

City finished off the month by beating Fulham 2-1 in the Carling Cup and comfortably seeing off West Ham 3-1 to make it seven wins out of the first eight games played. Things couldn't have been going better, but then inexplicably, with a run of games that looked – on paper – winnable, the Blues became locked in a cycle of drawing matches and recorded a record seven in succession.

The opposition included Wigan, Fulham, Burnley, Birmingham and Hull – all teams City needed to beat if the club was to be one of the Champions League hopefuls. Though a 5-1 win over Scunthorpe was sandwiched in that run and a 3-0 Carling Cup win over a young Arsenal side followed as the campaign drifted into December, the Blues had lost vital ground at the top.

An impressive 2-1 win over Chelsea proved that Hughes' team could compete with the best, but a sloppy defensive display at Bolton during a 3-3 draw was followed by the team's worst performance of the season at Tottenham with Harry Redknapp's side winning 3-0.

The momentum of the first few months had been lost and 25 goals had been shipped in 16 games. The club's owners were faced with a difficult decision, but the manner of the defeat at Spurs had been so disappointing that after another nervy display against Sunderland, when City won 4-3, Hughes was replaced as manager by former Inter Milan boss Roberto Mancini. >>

Season Review 2009/10

Mancini had won many trophies as a player and manager and was seen as the perfect man to take the club to the next level. His arrival coincided with a terrific run of form by Carlos Tevez who scored in each of Mancini's first three games in charge. Wins over Stoke City, Wolves and Blackburn – plus a 1-0 win over Middlesbrough in the FA Cup – gave the Italian boss the perfect start.

A 2-0 loss at a resurgent Everton was followed by an explosive Carling Cup semi-final against Manchester United. With City in the last four of a major competition for the first time in nearly 30 years, hopes were high as two Tevez goals gave the Blues a 2-1 first leg lead.

A 4-2 win over Scunthorpe (again) in the FA Cup took place before City again took on United in the second leg. With Robinho now back on loan in Brazil with Santos, the Blues were hoping for their first League Cup final since 1976, but despite Tevez levelling aggregates after United opened up a 2-0 lead, a last-gasp Wayne Rooney goal won the game 3-1 for the Reds and the Wembley dream was over.

A 2-0 win over Portsmouth was followed by a disappointing 2-1 defeat at Hull City, but at least new signings Patrick Vieira and Adam Johnson had decent games coming on off the bench. February proved to be patchy overall with the Hull loss followed by a 2-0 win over Bolton and three games

out of four with Stoke City – one in the league, two in the FA Cup. City won none of them and a 0-0 draw at home to Liverpool made Champions League qualification seem unlikely.

But City ended the month with their best display of the season – a 4-2 win at Chelsea thanks to two goals each from Bellamy and Tevez – to restore hopes of a top four finish. A 1-1 draw at Sunderland was followed by a slick 2-1 win at Fulham, but Everton repeated their January victory by ending City's unbeaten home record with a 2-0 win at the City of Manchester Stadium.

The Blues ended March and moved into April in top gear, easily beating Wigan 3-0, thrashing Burnley 6-1 and then destroying Birmingham City 5-1 to set up a clash with Manchester United at the City of Manchester Stadium.

With Spurs and Aston Villa right on City's coattails, nothing but a win would do against the Reds, but for the third time that season, United scored with virtually the last kick of the game. With Spurs then losing at United, the 0-0 draw at Arsenal meant that wins over Aston Villa and Spurs in the last two home games of the season would guarantee City finish fourth and win a place in the Champions League.

Sadly, it wasn't to be and Spurs won 2-0 to claim fourth. The final game of the season ended with a 1-1 draw at West Ham and City's players and fans were left to reflect on what might have been...

10 Things We Love About...

CARLOS

There are many more, but here are our favourite ten...

1 – His 29 goals during the 2009/10 season was the highest top flight total by a City player for 36 years!

2 – He scored three goals against Manchester United last season – a good reason to love him even more!

3 – His nickname is El Apache, partly because he was raised in the tough Argentinian neighbourhood of Fuerte Apache.

4 – His goal celebrations are never dull – his goal against Manchester United in the Carling Cup saw him sprint to the halfway line in front of Reds manager Sir Alex Ferguson and cup his hands behind his ears as the City fans sang 'Fergie, Fergie sign him up!'

5 – He scored one of the best goals of the 2010 World Cup with a 30-yard screamer against Mexico.

6 – He wears 32 in honour of one of his sporting heroes, basketball legend

TEVEZ

Michael Jordan, who used to wear the number 23 jersey – Tevez merely incorporated those numbers...

7 – Carlos scored two hat-tricks for City in his first season – one against Blackburn and another against Wigan that took just 10 minutes!!

8 – He was named the City fans' Player of the Year and was also voted Players' Player of the Year by his City team-mates – oh, and he was shortlisted for the PFA Player of the Year, too!

9 – He never gives in and nothing is a lost cause – he is the hardest working player on the pitch every time he plays.

10 – He never forgets his daughters when he plays and last season he produced shin pads with Katie and Flopy written on them when he celebrated scoring goals.

Location, Location

Can you guess the locations of the pictures below?

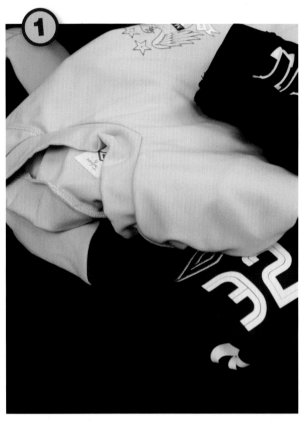

7
CITY ELITE
BEHAVIOURS.

★ ★ ★

Discipline

Team Spirit

Respect

Punctuality

Communication

Demand High Standards

Responsibility

M.C.F.C.

Created By The Players Of Team City

Answers on page 61

Who is Roberto Talking About?

Can you guess who the City boss is talking about? There are clues within each quote – see if you can work out who the mystery player is....

1 "It was a good performance. XXXXXXXX scored three important goals and we won this game. I am happy with him. He is scoring a lot of goals and has always been a good player. He is a young player, who is improving every year."

2 "If he continues like he is at the moment he could get into the national team. I remember Ryan Giggs when he was young and the way he moved. XXXXXXX is the same player. If he keeps working hard he has a good chance for the future."

3 "To score three goals, three very good goals, for us is very special but everyone knows how good he is. I wanted him to come to Inter. I asked about him but of course there was no chance because he was at Manchester United."

4 "XXXXXXXX is a good goalkeeper, who next year could be an important goalkeeper for England and Manchester City. He is only young and probably he will stay with us. But it is not an important issue just now. We must concentrate on our games and stick with what is happening this season."

Answers on page 61

ADAM JOHNSON

Spot the Difference

Picture A and Picture B are the same – or are they? Picture B actually has five slight differences – can you spot them all?

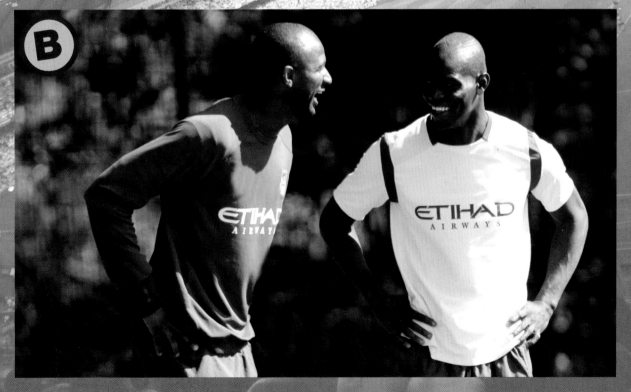

Answers on page 60

Match Day

The home dressing room prior to the Manchester Derby 2010

20 Pieces of Silva

David Silva became Roberto Mancini's second summer signing when he agreed to sign for the Blues from Valencia – here are 20 things you need to know

1, He was born as David Josué Jiménez Silva on the Canary Island of Gran Canaria on January 8, 1986.

2, His father is from Gran Canaria while his mother is of Japanese descent.

3, David's nickname is Cuco – at Valencia he was known as 'Wild Pony' because he was considered small in stature but with a strong will.

4, He can play on either the right or the left wing – just like Adam Johnson – and can also play as an attacking central midfielder.

5, At Valencia he wore the No.21 jersey – a shirt number that was unused at City last season.

6, David made his debut for Spain on 15 November 2006 against Romania.

7, He spent time on loan with two other Spanish sides while at Valencia – Celta Vigo and SD Eibar.

8, He scored his first goals for Spain against Greece in 2007, grabbing both Spanish goals in a 3-2 defeat.

9, As a young boy, he wanted to be a goalkeeper and his first strip was a keeper's outfit.

10, David is a shy lad and would rather stay out of the limelight, particularly not being comfortable with speaking in public.

11, He joined Valencia when he was aged 14.

12, David's favourite aftershave is Prada.

13, If he hadn't made it as a footballer, David would have liked to have been a surgeon – does this mean he was really good at the board game 'Operation'?

14, He was once the victim of an internet joke, when rumours circulated that he was a skilled machete fighter because of his half-Japanese background.

15, David has a younger brother, Nano, and a younger sister, Natalia.

16, His father Fernando was a safety officer at Valencia's stadium.

17, David had scored at the City of Manchester Stadium before he signed for the Blues – in August 2007 he scored Valencia's winning goal in a 1-0 pre-season friendly match.

18, He once scored a stunning goal away to Chelsea in the Champions League, beating Petr Cech from 30 yards.

19, He played in the same Spain Under-17 team as Cesc Fabregas.

20, At the time he joined City, he'd played 202 games and scored 32 goals. He'd also won 37 caps for Spain, scoring seven goals.

WORLDCUP2010
a World in Blue

BY THE END OF THE 2010 WORLD CUP THERE HAD BEEN 13 CITY PLAYERS IN ACTION AT SOME POINT DURING THE TOURNAMENT – HERE IS HOW EACH PLAYER DID

**JOE HART,
ENGLAND
PLAYED: 0
GOALS: 0**
Despite calls for him to get a game, Joe had to wait until after the World Cup to stake his claim to be England's No.1 – still, the experience will have done him good.

**ROQUE SANTA CRUZ,
PARAGUAY
PLAYED: 5
GOALS: 0**
Roque took part in all of Paraguay's games but couldn't find the net in any of them. Still troubled by knee problems, he didn't have the impact he perhaps would have liked.

**GARETH BARRY,
ENGLAND
PLAYED: 3
GOALS: 0**
Gareth only just made the England squad after being sidelined for a month with an ankle injury. Though he didn't let anyone down, he looked short of match fitness at times.

**SHAUN WRIGHT-PHILLIPS,
ENGLAND
PLAYED: 3
GOALS: 0**
Shaun had a great chance to score against the USA but shot straight at the keeper when clean through. He did OK when he came on but we didn't see any of his trademark weaving runs he does so often for City.

**KOLO TOURE,
IVORY COAST
PLAYED: 3
GOALS: 0**
Kolo's Ivory Coast were unfortunate to have Portugal and Brazil in the same group and the Elephants never really got going. Kolo played well and did what he could but his country went out in the group stages.

**YAYA TOURE,
IVORY COAST
PLAYED: 3
GOALS: 1**
Yaya managed to score a fine goal against North Korea but like his brother, would have been very disappointed not to have progressed to at least the Round of 16. He was not technically a City player during the World Cup but as good as!

**JAMES MILNER,
ENGLAND
PLAYED: 3
GOALS: 0**
In England's third match of the tournament, James setup the only goal of the game when his cross was converted by Jermain Defoe in the 1-0 win over Slovenia.

WORLDCUP2010
a World in Blue

ROBINHO,
BRAZIL
PLAYED: 4
GOALS: 2
A return to form by the Brazilian forward. With former City team-mate Elano alongside him, he looked like the player of old and took his two goals beautifully. He would have hoped to have gone all the way to the final but it wasn't to be.

CARLOS TEVEZ,
ARGENTINA
PLAYED: 4
GOALS: 2
Energetic and lively as ever, Tevez could have been one of the stars of the 2010 World Cup had Argentina progressed to the final. He scored one of the best goals of the competition with a brilliant strike against Mexico.

VLADIMIR WEISS,
SLOVAKIA
PLAYED: 3
GOALS: 0
He did well and looked comfortable on the wing – considering his age and lack of senior experience, he had an excellent World Cup.

DAVID SILVA,
SPAIN
PLAYED: 2
GOALS: 0
Underused by the Spain boss in many people's eyes, Silva was unfortunate to be part of the Spain side that lost to Switzerland. He will have many more opportunities in the future.

NIGEL DE JONG,
HOLLAND
PLAYED: 6
GOALS: 0
A typically industrious tournament by City's all-action midfielder. He tackled like his life depended on it and did the simple things, though was unfortunate to miss the semi-final through suspension.

JEROME BOATENG,
GERMANY
PLAYED: 5
GOALS: 0
Got better and better as the tournament progressed. Looked assured at the back and helped out in attack whenever he could. His star shone brightest against Argentina when he enjoyed a near faultless performance.

LOOK WHO'S TALKING

Here's what we reckon was being said when these pictures were taken...

"IT'S UP TO YOU, NEW YORK, NEW YORK!"

"RIO I HAD CABBAGE FOR DINNER, IS THERE ANY STUCK IN MY TEETH?"

"I'LL JUST CATCH A FEW RAYS WHILE WE DEFEND THIS CORNER..."

"BOSS, I TOLD YOU – THE CLOCKS WENT BACK LAST NIGHT, WE'RE TOO EARLY!"

"HEY IT'S TURNED OUT REALLY SOFT – TOLD YOU CONDITIONER HELPS..."

ALEKSANDAR KOLAROV

Wordsearch

Find the 10 names hidden in the grid. Words can go horizontally, vertically and diagonally in all eight directions.

MANCINI BOATENG BARRY ADEBAYOR ZABALETA JOHNSON TEVEZ LESCOTT BOYATA VIEIRA

```
Z E V E T B H T X J
Z R M M M V T V O W
A T B A A R Y H J I
B D V T Q M N R G N
A A E N T S P N R I
L T X B O O E X Z C
E A K N A T C K Z N
T Y B M A Y P S C A
A O L O W T O K E M
N B B V I E I R A L
```

Answers on page 61

DAVID SILVA

BehindtheScenes @Carrington

A sneak look at the players' secret world

Code of conduct board for younger players

Exercise bikes

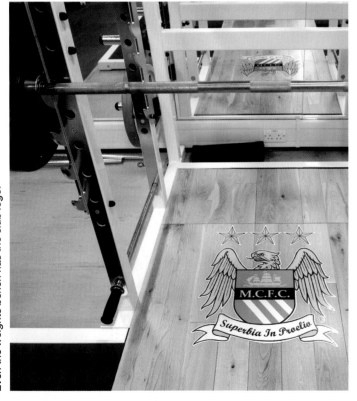

Even the weights bench has the club logo!

Changing rooms at Carrington

Lettering for the players' shirts

Boot room

(Above)
Gareth Barry in the gym

(Left)
A relaxed warm-down session

THE BIG CITY QUIZ

2011

Time to test your knowledge of the Blues

1, DURING THE 2010 WORLD CUP, HOW MANY GOALS DID CARLOS TEVEZ SCORE AGAINST MEXICO?

2, WHICH CLUB DID ADAM JOHNSON JOIN CITY FROM?

3, WHICH MONTH DID ROBERTO MANCINI TAKE OVER AS CITY MANAGER IN 2009?

4, WHO KNOCKED CITY OUT OF THE 2009/10 FA CUP?

5, WHICH TEAM DID SYLVINHO SCORE HIS ONLY GOAL FOR CITY AGAINST?

6, WHICH TEAM DID CITY PLAY IN THE FINAL HOME GAME OF THE SEASON?

7, THE BLUES' BIGGEST WIN OF SEASON 2009/10 WAS 6-1 – BUT WHO WAS IT AGAINST?

8, CITY'S FIFTH PLACE FINISH IN THE 2009/10 SEASON WAS THE CLUB'S HIGHEST EVER IN THE PREMIER LEAGUE. TRUE OR FALSE?

9, WHICH CLUB DID JOE HART SPEND THE 2009/10 SEASON ON LOAN WITH?

10, WHO WAS VOTED CITY'S PLAYER OF THE YEAR FOR 2009/10?

11, WHO DID ADAM JOHNSON MAKE HIS ENGLAND DEBUT AGAINST?

12, WHICH TWO PREMIER LEAGUE CLUBS BEAT CITY BOTH HOME AND AWAY DURING THE 2009/10 SEASON?

13, FOUR DIFFERENT GOALKEEPERS PLAYED FOR CITY DURING THE 2009/10 CAMPAIGN – WHO WERE THEY?

14, FROM WHICH CLUB DID YAYA TOURE JOIN CITY FROM?

15, NIGEL DE JONG JOINED CITY FROM DUTCH GIANTS AJAX. TRUE OR FALSE?

16, WHO DID CITY BEAT 4-3 AT HOME IN 2009/10?

17, OUT OF THESE THREE ENGLAND GOALKEEPERS, WHO IS THE ODD ONE OUT – JOE HART, DAVID JAMES OR ROBERT GREEN?

18, WHO DID ROBINHO SPEND PART OF THE 2009/10 SEASON ON LOAN TO?

19, WHO DID CITY RESERVES BEAT TO WIN THE 2009/10 MANCHESTER SENIOR CUP?

20, WHICH NUMBER DOES CARLOS TEVEZ WEAR FOR CITY?

Answers on page 61

GARETH BARRY

Guess Who?

1

2

Can you work out who these City players are?

3

4

New Blue: Yaya Toure

Yaya Toure joined City from Barcelona during the summer after signing a five year contract.

The Ivory Coast midfielder left the La Liga champions and linked up with his older brother Kolo – the last brothers to play for City were Shaun and Bradley Wright-Phillips.

Yaya played at the 2010 World Cup, playing every game for his country and scoring once. At the time he joined City, he had won 49 caps for Ivory Coast.

Yaya is very tall for a midfielder standing at 6 feet 2 inches – he is expected to play a 'holding' role for the Blues meaning that he will play just in front of the defence and his job will be to break up the attacks of the team City are playing.

He was a very popular figure among the Barcelona supporters and had attracted interest from a number of top clubs in the Premier League and around Europe.

He decided the team he wanted to join was City – perhaps convinced by his big brother – and he could well be one of the best signings of the summer.

Yaya, one of three footballing brothers, began his career as a youth with Ivorian side ASEC Mimosas in 1996 before he moved to Beveren aged 18 in 2001, spending two full seasons with the Belgian side before joining Ukrainian side Metaluhr Donetsk in 2003.

After spells with Greek side Olympiacos and Monaco in France enhanced his reputation yet further, Yaya became the first Ivorian to be signed by Barcelona who paid around £9m for his services in 2007.

In 2009, he won the Champions League with the Catalonian side as an emergency centre-half and he celebrated his second successive La Liga title with Barca last May before jetting off to South Africa – his second World Cup, having been part of the 2006 Ivory Coast squad in Germany.

After 118 appearances with Barcelona and a total of almost 300 career appearances in total, City have signed a very experienced, very talented footballer.

His hero as a young player was Patrick Vieira and he wore the No.24 shirt for Barca in his honour. He may have a battle for the same squad number at City, however – the Blues' current No.24 is none other than Patrick Vieira!

Crossword

See if you can fill the puzzle by answering the clues below...

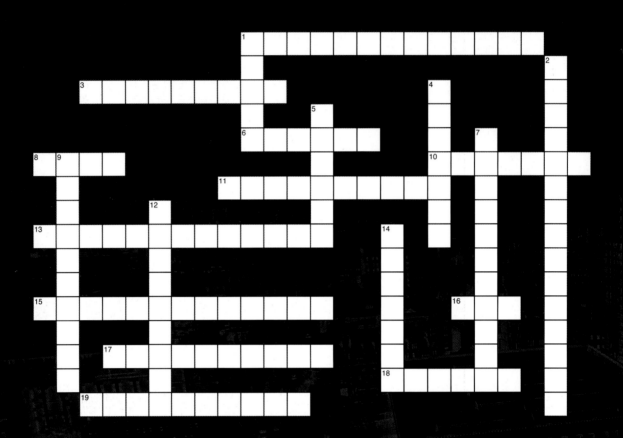

ACROSS

1 Who did Carlos Tevez score his first City hat-trick against? (5,8)
3 Former club legend who has a stand named after him. (5,4)
6 Brazilian club Robinho joined on loan. (6)
8 The number of goals City scored against Scunthorpe last season. (4)
10 The team Joleon Lescott joined City from. (7)
11 What is the name of City's kit manager? (3,7)
13 Carlos Tevez's first English club. (4,3,6)
15 Club Adam Johnson joined City from. (13)
16 Number of goals City scored against Manchester United in 2009/10 season. (3)
17 The country Kolo and Yaya Toure represent. (5,5)
18 Shay Given never plays in goal without a pair of these! (6)
19 The team Adam Johnson scored his first City goal against. (10)

DOWN

1 Country Craig Bellamy has captained. (5)
2 Which club did Martin Petrov join after leaving City? (6,9)
4 The only other English club Patrick Vieira has played for. (7)
5 Name of City's shirt sponsors. (6)
7 The first names of Jerome Boateng's brother. (5,6)
9 Which club did Roberto Mancini manage before City? (5,5)
12 The name of City's home up until 2003. (5,4)
14 The club Jerome Boateng, Nigel de Jong and Vincent Kompany all joined City from. (7)

JOLEON LESCOTT

Goal!

Get in! 10 cracking goals from the 2009/10 season

1, ADAM JOHNSON V SUNDERLAND

With just minutes remaining, Johnson cut back on to his left foot on the edge of the box, looked up and then curled a sweet shot into the top corner of the net.

2, EMMANUEL ADEBAYOR V ARSENAL

It just had to happen – with so much talk before the game of Ade and his unhappy last few months at Arsenal, you just knew he'd score. He rose like a salmon to bury a header past Almunia.

3, CRAIG BELLAMY V MANCHESTER UNITED

Bellamy picked the ball up on the left and headed towards the United box. He dropped his shoulder, cut inside and unleashed a rocket shot that flew into the top corner to silence Old Trafford.

4, CRAIG BELLAMY V MANCHESTER UNITED

With just a minute or so of normal time remaining, Bellamy was put through by Martin Petrov near the halfway line following a Rio Ferdinand mistake. He raced clear, took it round the keeper and slotted home.

5, SYLVINHO V SCUNTHORPE

The Brazilian defender picked the ball up in midfield and with nobody closing him down, carried on forward before unleashing a rocket shot from 30 yards that flew in.

6, CARLOS TEVEZ
V ARSENAL

Tevez moved into the box, beat two players before unleashing a ferocious drive that struck the underside of the bar and bounced up into the roof of the net – fantastic!

7, CARLOS TEVEZ
V FULHAM

After winning the ball on the halfway line, Tevez played the ball to Craig Bellamy who raced down the left before chipping the ball back to Tevez who chested the ball down, raced into the box and then stroked the ball home after leaving defenders aside and the keeper on his backside.

8, CARLOS TEVEZ
V WIGAN

His third in 12 minutes, this was also his best. He beat three Wigan players, drew the keeper off his line before cracking a rising shot into the back of the net. Genius!

9, CARLOS TEVEZ
V BLACKBURN ROVERS

With City rampant, Gareth Barry nodded the ball across the Blackburn six-yard box. It appeared to be just out of reach of Tevez until he made an acrobatic lunge to get the merest of touches past keeper Paul Robinson and into the net.

10, CRAIG BELLAMY
V CHELSEA

Gareth Barry chipped the ball into Bellamy's path on the halfway line and the quicksilver forward left his marker chasing shadows before running into the box and slotting the ball past Hilario.

Design Your Own Boots

Ever thought 'I can do better than that' or not been able to find the boots that suit your particular taste? Well now you have the chance to design your very own boots. Select the colours you need and don't forget to choose a name for them, too...

Dream 11

City are often linked with the best players in the world and have many of them at the club already – but if you were manager, who would you choose? We've set out a team below and all you have to do is select either your dream team or your favourite eleven from the current squad – you're the boss – you decide!

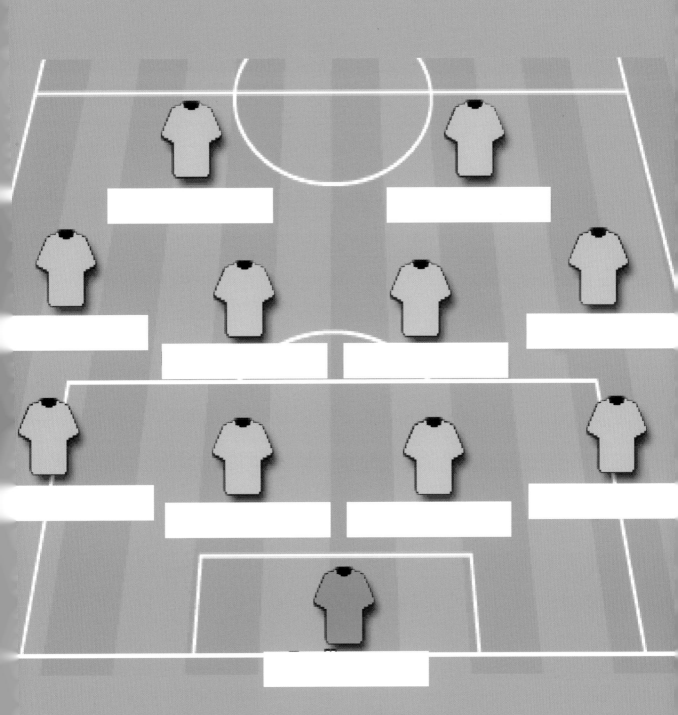

New Blue:
Jerome Boateng

He was one of the unsung heroes of Germany's 2010 World Cup campaign – now discover 10 facts about City's new defender Jerome Boateng...

1, Jerome was born in Berlin-Wilmersdorf in Germany on September 3, 1988.

2, His mother is German but his father is Ghanaian. Jerome elected to play for his mum's birth nation while his brother Kevin-Prince chose Ghana. The pair met in the 2010 World Cup creating history as the first brothers to oppose each other in the competition.

3, Jerome's parents had interesting jobs when he was small – his mum was an air hostess and his dad a DJ!

4, He made his debut for Germany in October 2009 against Russia – and was sent off for two bookable offences!

5, He chose the No.17 shirt for his first season with City.

6, Jerome is believed to have cost City in excess of £10m.

7, He has four tattoos – one with his middle name 'Agyenim' included within it – a Ghanaian word for The Great One!

8, Jerome is the third Hamburg player to join City in the last two years following in the footsteps of Vincent Kompany and Nigel de Jong.

9, Apart from Kevin-Prince, Jerome has one sister, Avelina, and another brother, George - though not the Hull City and former Middlesbrough player of the same name!

10, Don't expect too many goals from Jerome – he never managed to find the net during his three years and 75 appearances with Hamburg...

Guess Who?

We've disguised five City players here, can you write in their missing names in the boxes attached?

Answers on page 60

VINCENT KOMPANY

Spot the Ball

A   B   C   D   E   F

1
2
3
4
5
6
7
8

Answer on page 60

MANCHESTER CITY FC
Squad Profiles 2011

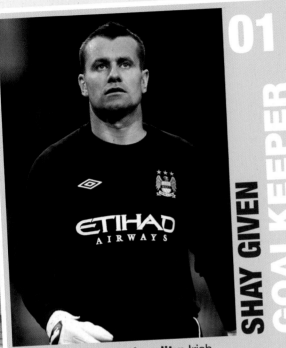

01

SHAY GIVEN GOALKEEPER

Born: 20/04/76 **Nationality:** Irish
Previous clubs: Celtic, Blackburn Rovers, Swindon Town (loan), Sunderland (loan), Newcastle Utd **Career highlight:** Becoming Ireland's most capped goalkeeper when he earned his 100th cap and captained his country

25

JOE HART GOALKEEPER

Born: 19/04/87 **Nationality:** English
Previous clubs: Shrewsbury Town, Tranmere (loan), Blackpool (loan), Birmingham City (loan)
Career highlight: Winning first England cap v Trinidad & Tobago in 2008 and being voted Birmingham City's Player of the Year 2010

12

STUART TAYLOR GOALKEEPER

Born: 28/11/1980 **Nationality:** English
Previous clubs: Arsenal, Bristol Rovers (loan) Crystal Palace (loan) Peterborough (loan), Leicester (loan) Aston Villa, Cardiff (loan)
Career highlight: Premier League champions medal winner

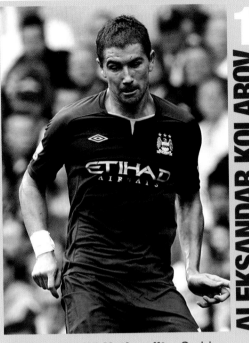

13

ALEKSANDAR KOLAROV
DEFENDER

Born: 10/11/85 **Nationality:** Serbian
Previous clubs: Cukaricki Stankhom,
OFK, Lazio
Career highlight: Winning first cap for Serbia
in 2008

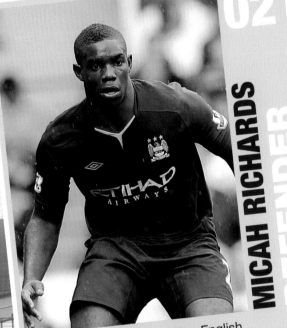

02

MICAH RICHARDS
DEFENDER

Born: 24/06/88 **Nationality:** English
Previous clubs: Academy graduate
Career highlight: Scoring for England v
Israel at Wembley in 2007

05

PABLO ZABALETA
DEFENDER

Born: 16/01/85 **Nationality:** Argentinian
Previous clubs: San Lorenzo, Espanyol
Career highlight: Winning gold medal for
Argentina at 2008 Olympics

MANCHESTER CITY FC
Squad Profiles 2011

03

WAYNE BRIDGE
DEFENDER

Born: 05/08/80 **Nationality:** English
Previous clubs: Southampton, Chelsea, Fulham (loan)
Career highlight: Winning first England cap v Holland in 2002

28

KOLO TOURE
DEFENDER

Born: 19/03/81 **Nationality:** Ivorian
Previous clubs: Arsenal
Career highlight: Representing Ivory Coast at 2010 World Cup

44

DEDRYCK BOYATA
DEFENDER

Born: 28/11/90 **Nationality:** Belgian
Previous clubs: Academy graduate
Career highlight: Making senior debut for City v Middlesbrough in the January 2010 FA Cup win

22

GREG CUNNINGHAM
DEFENDER

Born: 31/01/91 **Nationality:** Irish
Previous clubs: Academy graduate
Career highlight: Making debut for Ireland v Paraguay in 2010

17

JEROME BOATENG
DEFENDER

Born: 03/09/88 **Nationality:** German
Previous clubs: Hamburg
Career highlight: Representing Germany at 2010 World Cup

MANCHESTER CITY FC
Squad Profiles 2011

19

JOLEON LESCOTT
DEFENDER

Born: 16/08/82 **Nationality:** English
Previous clubs: Wolves, Everton
Career highlight: Making England debut

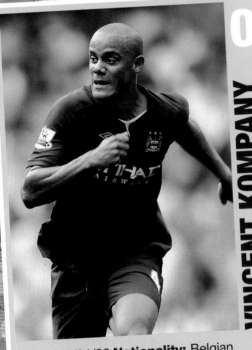

04

VINCENT KOMPANY
DEFENDER

Born: 10/04/86 **Nationality:** Belgian
Previous clubs: Anderlecht, Hamburg
Career highlight: International debut for
Belgium v France in 2004 aged 18

06

MICHAEL JOHNSON
MIDFIELDER

Born: 24/02/88 **Nationality:** English
Previous clubs: Academy graduate
Career highlight: Making England Under-21
debut

48

ABDISALAM IBRAHIM MIDFIELDER

Born: 01/05/91 **Nationality**: Norwegian (born in Somalia) **Previous clubs:** Fjellhamar **Career highlight:** Making senior debut for City v Scunthorpe in January 2010

34

NIGEL DE JONG MIDFIELDER

Born: 30/11/84 **Nationality:** Dutch **Previous clubs:** Ajax, Hamburg **Career highlight:** International debut for Holland v France in 2004

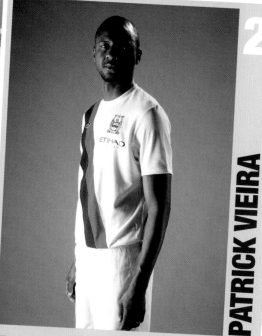

24

PATRICK VIEIRA MIDFIELDER

Born: 23/06/76 **Nationality:** French **Previous clubs:** Arsenal, Juventus, Inter Milan **Career highlight:** Winning the 1998 World Cup with France

MANCHESTER CITY FC
Squad Profiles 2011

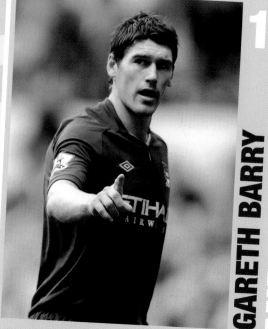

18

GARETH BARRY MIDFIELDER

Born: 23/02/81 **Nationality:** English
Previous clubs: Brighton, Aston Villa
Career highlight: First England cap v Ukraine in 2002

08

SHAUN WRIGHT-PHILLIPS MIDFIELDER

Born: 25/10/81 **Nationality:** English
Previous clubs: Chelsea
Career highlight: Scoring on his England debut v Ukraine in 2004 and playing at 2010 World Cup

07

JAMES MILNER MIDFIELDER

Born: 04/01/86 **Nationality:** English
Previous clubs: Leeds, Swindon (loan), Newcastle, Aston Villa
Career highlight: Winning first England 'Senior' cap v Holland in 200

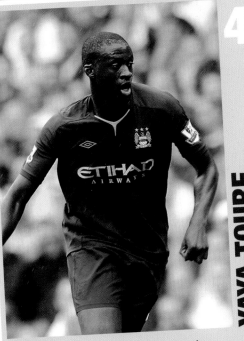

42

YAYA TOURE
MIDFIELDER

Born: 13/05/83 **Nationality:** Ivorian
Previous clubs: Beveren, Metaluhr Donetsk, Olympiacos, Monaco, Barcelona
Career highlight: Winning 2009 Champions League with Barcelona

40

VLADIMIR WEISS
MIDFIELDER

Born: 30/11/89 **Nationality:** Slovakian
Previous clubs: Bolton Wanderers (loan)
Career highlight: Playing for Slovakia at 2010 World Cup

11

ADAM JOHNSON
MIDFIELDER

Born: 14/07/87 **Nationality:** English
Previous clubs: Middlesbrough
Career highlight: Making England debut v Mexico in June 2010

14

ROQUE SANTA CRUZ
FORWARD

Born: 16/8/1981 **Nationality:** Paraguayan
Previous clubs: Olimpia, Bayern Munich, Blackburn
Career highlight: Voted Paraguayan Footballer of the Year in 1999. Won 61 caps for his country

21

DAVID SILVA
MIDFIELDER

Born: 08/01/86 **Nationality:** Spanish
Previous clubs: Valencia, Eibar (loan), Celta Vigo (loan)
Career highlight: Scoring two goals for Spain v Greece in August 2007

10

ROBINHO
FORWARD

Born: 25/01/84 **Nationality:** Brazilian
Previous clubs: Santos, Real Madrid, Santos (loan)
Career highlight: First cap for Brazil v Mexico in 2003

45

MARIO BALOTELLI
FORWARD

Born: 12/08/90 **Nationality:** Italian
Previous clubs: Inter Milan
Career highlight: Making full debut for Italy in August 2010 v Ivory Coast

25

EMMANUEL ADEBAYOR
FORWARD

Born: 24/02/84 **Nationality:** Togolese
Previous clubs: Metz, Monaco, Arsenal
Career highlight: Being voted African Footballer of the Year 2008

32

CARLOS TEVEZ
FORWARD

Born: 05/02/84 **Nationality:** Argentinian
Previous clubs: West Ham United, Manchester United
Career highlight: Winning 50th cap for Argentina

Quiz Answers

Spot the Difference (From Page 17)

Guess Who? (From page 35)

1, Joleon Lescott
2, David Silva
3, Kolo Toure
4, Carlos Tevez

Guess Who? (From page 46)

1 Shay Given

2 David Silva

3 Nigel De Jong

4 Gareth Barry

5 Micah Richards

Spot the Ball (From page 48)

Answer F1

BIG CITY QUIZ - ANSWERS
(From page 32)

1, Two

2, Middlesbrough

3, December

4, Stoke City

5, Scunthorpe

6, Tottenham

7, Burnley

8, True

9, Birmingham

10, Carlos Tevez

11, Mexico

12, Tottenham & Everton

13, Shay Given, Stuart Taylor, Gunnar Nielsen and Marton Fullop

14, Barcelona

15, False – he signed from Hamburg

16, Sunderland

17, Robert Green – both James and Hart have played for City

18, Santos

19, Bolton Wanderers

20, No.32

LOCATION, LOCATION
(From page 14)

1, Laundry room, Carrington

2, Boot room, Carrington

3, Locker rooms, Carrington

WHO IS ROBERTO TALKING ABOUT?
(From page 15)

1, Carlos Tevez

2, Adam Johnson

3, Carlos Tevez

4, Joe Hart

WORDSEARCH
(From page 28)

CROSSWORD SOLUTION (From page 38)